HANDWRITING PRACTICE 5TH GRADE

CHILDREN'S READING & WRITING EDUCATION BOOKS

PROFESSOR GUSTO
EDUCATIONAL & INFORMATIVE BOOKS FOR CHILDREN
(PRE-K / K-12)

All Rights reserved. No part of this book may be reproduced or used in any way or form or by any means whether electronic or mechanical, this means that you cannot record or photocopy any material ideas or tips that are provided in this book

Copyright 2016

Trace and rewrite the words in the space provided.

baptism   baptism

criticism   criticism

cubism   cubism

elitism   elitism

biblical   biblical

clerical   clerical

clinical   clinical

cyclical   cyclical

ethical   ethical

magical   magical

physical   physical

criteria   criteria

hysteria	hysteria
inertia	inertia
phobia	phobia
tourism	tourism

couple   couple

example   example

people   people

triple   triple

abusively abusively

actively actively

armful armful

beautiful beautiful

careful   careful

cheerful   cheerful

mission   mission

session   session

ultimate   ultimate

unique   unique

unkind   unkind

upward   upward

version

vertical

vehicle

variety

winner winner

winter winter

tackle tackle

tablet tablet

safety safety

satisfy satisfy

scissors scissors

scratch scratch

senate   senate

language   language

launch   launch

leather   leather

abandon abandon

ability ability

science science

advance advance

before	before
believe	believe
cabinet	cabinet
camera	camera

earth	earth
eastern	eastern
eight	eight
electric	electric

elevator / elevator

emotion / emotion

enable / enable

engine / engine

flower   flower

follow   follow

fortune fortune

forward forward

gentle   gentle

genuine   genuine

general   general

hammer   hammer

handle   handle

quality   quality

range   range

record   record

release release

package package

planet planet

cabinet cabinet

Trace and rewrite the quotes in the space provided.

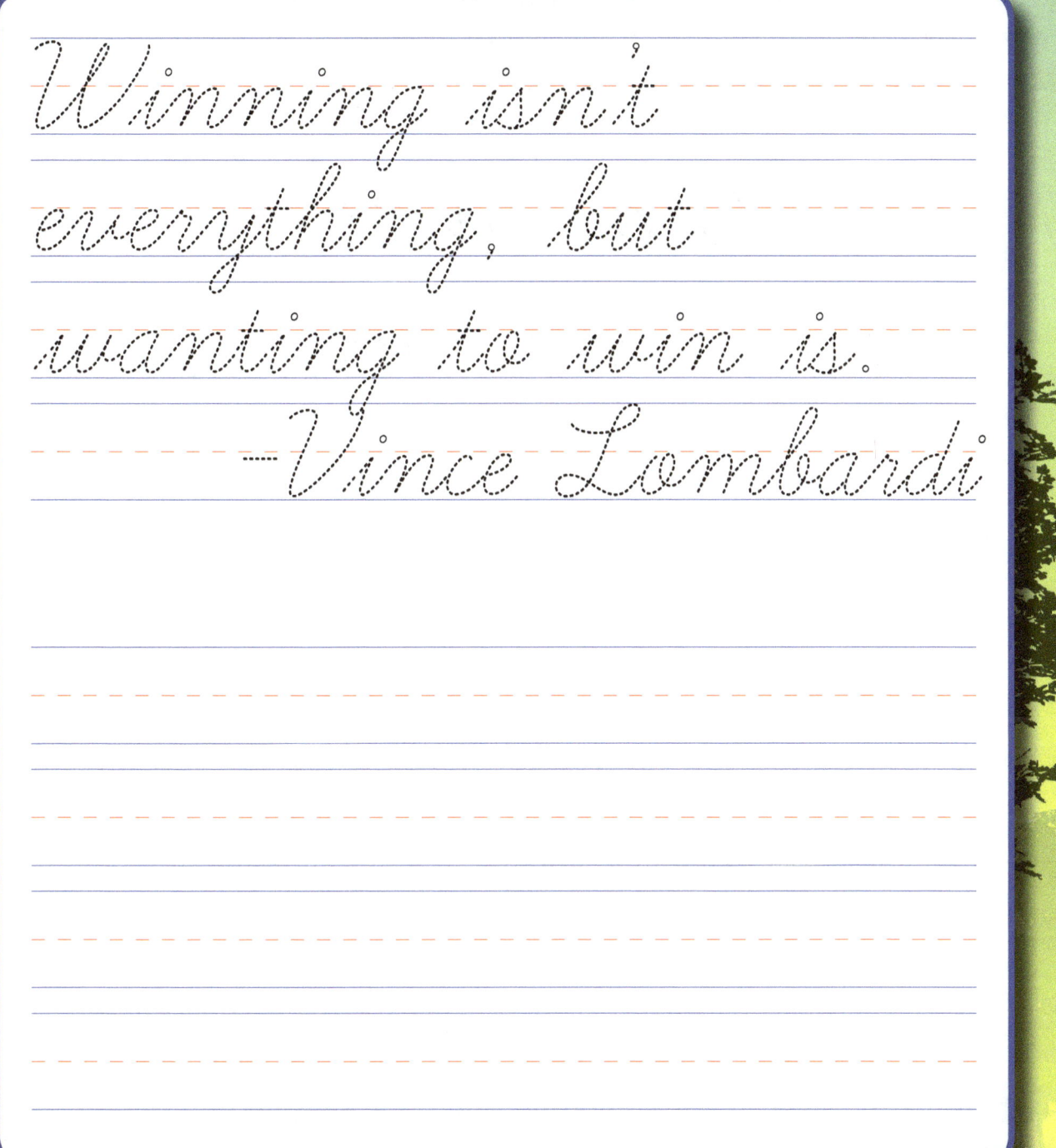

Winning isn't everything, but wanting to win is.
—Vince Lombardi

Every strike brings me closer to the next home run.
—Babe Ruth

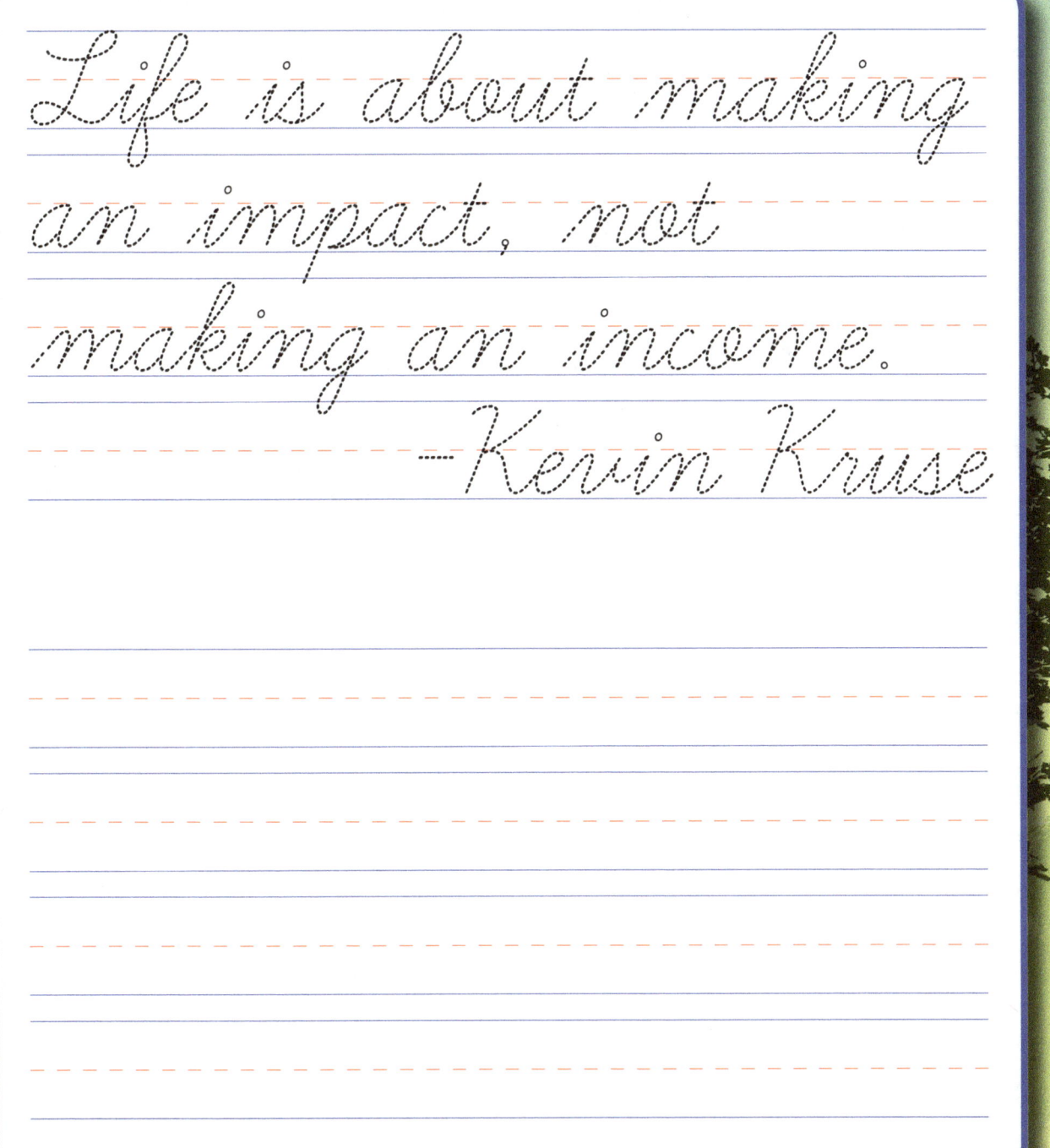

Life is about making an impact, not making an income.
—Kevin Kruse

Strive not to be a success, but rather to be of value.
—Albert Einstein

> To live a creative life,
> we must lose our
> fear of being wrong.
> — Anonymous

No one can make you feel inferior without your consent.
—Eleanor Roosevelt

Don't raise your voice, improve your argument.

—Anonymous

No masterpiece was ever created by a lazy artist.

—Anonymous

The starting point of all achievement is desire.

—Napolean Hill

You may have to fight a battle more than once to win it.
— Margaret Thatcher

You must be the change you wish to see in the world.

— Gandhi

Sometimes I worry about being a success in a mediocre world.
—Lily Tomlin

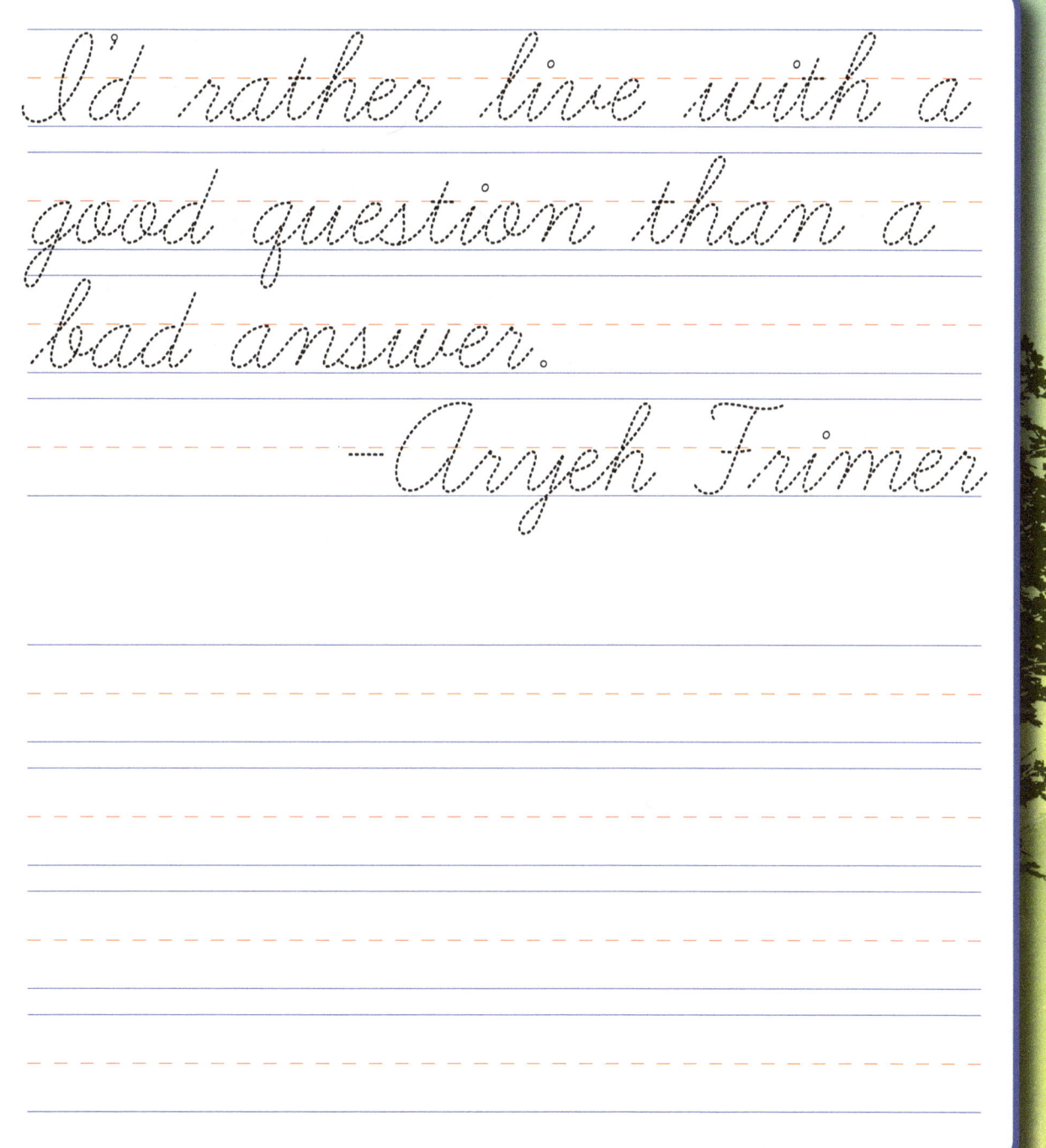

I'd rather live with a good question than a bad answer.
—Aryeh Frimer

You can do anything, but not everything.
—David Allen

You miss 100 percent of the shots you never take.
—Wayne Gretzky

www.ingramcontent.com/pod-product-compliance
Lightning Source LLC
LaVergne TN
LVHW061323060426
835507LV00019B/2269